The Kite Rider

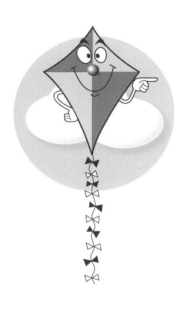

Contents

OXFORD
UNIVERSITY PRESS

Great Clarendon Street, Oxford OX2 6DP

Oxford University Press is a department of the University of Oxford.
It furthers the University's objective of excellence in research, scholarship,
and education by publishing worldwide in

Oxford   New York

Auckland   Cape Town   Dar es Salaam   Hong Kong   Karachi
Kuala Lumpur   Madrid   Melbourne   Mexico City   Nairobi
New Delhi   Shanghai   Taipei   Toronto

With offices in

Argentina   Austria   Brazil   Chile   Czech Republic   France   Greece
Guatemala   Hungary   Italy   Japan   South Korea   Poland   Portugal
Singapore   Switzerland   Thailand   Turkey   Ukraine   Vietnam

Oxford is a registered trade mark of Oxford University Press
in the UK and in certain other countries

British Library Cataloguing in Publication Data

Data available

ISBN-13: 978-0-19-832654-0

ISBN-10: 0-19-832654-8

10 9 8 7 6 5 4 3 2 1

Printed in Malaysia by Imago.

Acknowledgements

P4t OUP; **p4m** Free Agents Limited/Corbis; **p6** Reed Kaestne/Corbis; **p7** Yann Arthus-Mertran/Corbis; **p8** Topfoto.co.uk; **p9** Mark A Johnson/Corbis; **p11** Robert Wallis/Corbis; **p13t** Corel/OUP; **p13b** akg-images; **p14t** Dennis Galante/Corbis; **p14b** Karen Su/Corbis; **p15t** Bettmann/Corbis; **p15b** Barry Lewis/Corbis.

Illustrations are by John Hallett **pp Kites, 4b**; Annabel Large **pp7, 10, 12, 14**.

We are grateful for permission to reprint the following copyright
material in this guide:

James Fenton: 'Tianenmen' from *Out of Danger* (Penguin, 1993),
copyright © James Fenton 1993, used by permission of PFD on behalf of
James Fenton.

Geraldine McCaughrean: letter used by permission of the author.

We have tried to trace and contact all copyright holders before
publication. If notified, the publisher will be pleased to rectify any
errors or omissions at the earliest opportunity.

Key to icons:

 Pair or group activity

 A resources sheet from the Teacher's Pack supports this activity.

A Letter from Geraldine McCaughrean

Dear Reader,

I was riding on a tube train when it stopped alongside an advert for an exhibition at the Victoria and Albert Museum. It talked about 'Japanese kites large enough to carry a man', and I found myself picturing how it would be to ride a kite through the sky. By the time I was free to begin writing, the exhibition had gone and research produced nothing about Japanese man-carrying kites. But I did read about Marco Polo who, in China, saw a man tied to the hatch-cover of a ship and flown above it to discover whether the ship would meet with good luck or bad. 'That'll do!' I thought.

Isn't there something both wonderful and terrifying about the idea of flying? Once upon a time, I started to learn to fly light aeroplanes and got as far as flying solo… but I must admit I was terrified most of the time.

When I start a book I have no idea what it will turn out to be 'about' – I just try for an exciting adventure. But themes always do arise, somehow. 'Obedience' crops up a lot during *The Kite Rider*.

When I was a child, I had to do exactly as I was told – no choice. And yet by the time I got a daughter of my own, the world had changed so much that she wasn't bound by the same rules. In fact she thinks I should do as I'm told! Society no longer says, 'Children do as your parents say.' And yet in times past and in countries like China, a parent could KILL a child for the sin of disobedience! So while I was writing, I was thinking a lot about the rights and wrongs of doing what you are told. (I think I decided that obedience has to be earned.) See if it shows.

I really hope you enjoy reading *The Kite Rider* and that your feet leave the ground for a while at least.

Focus on China

Take away a taste of Haoyou's China and test your knowledge of the book!

Check out the true/false questions here. See how many you get right!

The Chinese were there First!

Over 80 years before Columbus, the 15th-century Chinese explorer, Cheng Ho made voyages to explore the Western world. He sailed in the multi-masted sailing ships or 'junks' featured in *The Kite Rider,* which the Chinese probably invented in about 200 AD.

Down at the waterfront

What was it like when Gou Pei and Haoyou arrived at Dagu's harbour? With a partner imagine that you are watching as the ships are loaded with cargo and the Jade Circus disembarks. One of you is a local and the other a visitor from another town.

- ◉ The visitor shuts his or her eyes while the local describes the scene like a guided tour capturing the sights, sounds and smells of the waterfront.
- ◉ Now reverse roles, explaining the harbour scene during Pei's fateful flight.

Tasty take-away?

The real McCoy comes from a variety of different Chinese regions and much of it is served with rice – it is said to be bad manners to leave one grain of rice in your bowl!

Sichuan cuisine is spicy and there are great dishes such as 'bang-bang chicken'.

Cantonese cuisine invented stir-fry, partly to conserve energy and partly to avoid over-cooking. However, apparently they're not fussy about what they include – snakes, bears' paws, turtles, weasels, rabbits, dogs, cats…

Fancy a cup of *cha*?

Tea or *cha* is drunk everywhere in China, especially at meal times. As well as Western tea there are many flower teas such chrysanthemum or *juhua cha.*

Feng Shui

Feng Shui is a way of making sure that the site of a building, its design and contents are favourable for the happiness and prosperity of everyone who lives there. It is based on ancient Taoist beliefs and the idea that the natural flow of energy or chi is influenced by the balance of the five basic elements (earth, fire, metal, water and wood), and yin and yang.
These are the opposing forces of light/dark, sun/moon, male/female, summer/winter.

Good luck charm

Models of sailing ships loaded with money were sometimes placed at the doors of houses in China, pointing inwards to bring good fortune to the owner.

With a group of your friends, select four objects which you think are important to one of the characters in the novel, such as Little Dog Wu or Miao Jié's white whip.

- ◉ Draw them roughly on pieces of paper.
- ◉ Discuss why you think these are important in the story.
- ◉ One of you sits in role as the chosen character, with the others placing the pieces of paper with the objects in the position you think would bring the most happiness and prosperity for that character.
- ◉ Offer your explanation as you place your object or alter the position of any objects already placed if you want.

Following a path...

The Chinese are deeply philosophical and religious.
Confucianism is a philosophy of social behaviour. It teaches duty and obedience to family elders.

Quick Quiz

1 Pei's sailing ship was renamed when the Mongols came to power.
True or false? (Chapter 1)
2 The performers in the Jade Circus drink fermented mare's milk and eat goats' meat. True or false? (Chapters 8 and 11)
3 The Mighty Khan does not believe in the Chinese tradition of Feng Shui. True or false? (Chapter 14)
4 Miao Jié is a Confucian. True or false? (page 15)

4 True. Miao Jié is a Confucian. (page 141)
3 False. Aniko, a Tibetan, is designing him a Buddhist temple for his park in Dadu. (page 132)
2 True. Most of the circus is made up of Mongols and this is their diet. (pages 71 and 102)
1 True. The ship was renamed 'Chabi' after the Khan's favourite wife. (page 2)
Answers

From Seaman's Son to Sun Swallow

'Oh, Haoyou. Be glad the gods gave you the gift of clever hands,' she said. *'They certainly held back on the brains.'*

A **tajik** or city-dweller, a keeper-to-one-place, Haoyou is thrown into a turbulent new life. He will need his wits about him, but our hero has plenty of courage. What dangers will he face?

Compiling a file on Haoyou

Act as a detective to uncover all the info on Haoyou. As you read the novel, add details to your file and piece together the secrets of Haoyou's personality.

Quick Quiz

Read Chapters 1 and 2.
1 What is Haoyou's family name?
2 Where does he live and with whom?
3 What does he wear?
4 What is his favourite possession?

> A woman needs a friendly face at a time like this. *(page 8)*

> I'll sew you a tiger on your jacket. A new tiger... *(page 14)*

> I won't fail... *(page 30)*

Remember ...
- **You'll need to go back to the text for each part.**
- **You'll learn more about other characters and events too.**

City to circus (Chapters 1 to 7)

When his father dies, Haoyou is pulled in different directions, under pressure from various people. Match the sentences up with the correct characters.
- What does Haoyou think about each person?
- What does this tell us about him?

Di Chou is a villain. Haoyou feels protective of his mother and is not taken in by him.

Giddy heights, sweeping lows (Chapters 8–14)

Match the excerpts on page 7 with the correct events.
- What was Haoyou thinking about?
- What do we learn about him from each excerpt?

Haoyou is still a child. He needs his mother and words of comfort to reassure him.

... like the corner of his mother's apron on bath night...

(page 75)

... cousin, you are twelve kinds of a fool.

(page 77)

The worst fear of all...

(page 89)

If those birds were just free...

(page 93)

'But it was a trick! We tricked them!'

(page 87)

The start of a romance?

Losing his courage

Leaving a mother

A lost child

Talking to the spirits

Dog or Gou was Haoyou's family name. Sewn on his padded jacket, Little Dog Wu is a constant reminder of home.

Bo's your uncle! (Chapters 15–22)

Match up the excerpts with Haoyou's qualities.

◉   Where else in the book does he show these?

Haoyou is growing up and challenging his childhood beliefs.

◉   How does he feel about Great Uncle Bo and his family now?

◉   What about his father's spirit?

Haoyou dared to persist.

(page 146)

... there was a kind of joy in the extra pang of fear...

(page 151)

Haoyou the traitor.

(page 170)

'I wouldn't have minded!... If I could have gone on flying for you.'

(page 164)

'It was a blackberry stain, a scorchmark, a tiny tear in the stretched white fabric of Life.'

(page 188)

Loyal and self sacrificing

Challenging authority

Surviving tragedy

Guilty and responsible

Enjoying a flight

'Qing'an bent, and swung Wawa up on to her hip'

Haoyou measure up...

How many of these qualities do you have? Score yourself from 1 to 10 on each and compare with a partner.

Up, Up and Away...

The word for kite in China is *fen zheng* – *fen* is wind and *zheng* is a stringed musical instrument.

Check out Cathay's Kites!

Kite-flying in China has a long and ancient tradition going back over 3000 years. It became popular during the Sung dynasty before the Mongol occupation and the action in our story. Originally Chinese kites were probably made of silk and bamboo, whereas those from Malaysia and Indonesia were made from leaves. However, kite-flying soon spread via the trade routes such as the silk road, to Arabia, Africa and Europe.

The Chinese were the first to write about kite-flying and there are many stories about their invention – from a hat being blown off, to the wind filling boat sails. Later there were tales about kites being used for entering enemy territory or making noises to frighten the enemy. The famous 13th-century Venetian traveller to China, Marco Polo (often credited for bringing pasta to Italy!) described how merchants used a fool or a drunkard tied to a kite, to test the wind before a ship set sail.

Once paper was invented, the construction of kites became popular all over the world and started the human fascination with flying which eventually brought us the aeroplane.

Why fly the skies?

Haoyou flew the wind for all sorts of different reasons. Look at the timeline below and see if you can make your own, filling in each flight Haoyou made as you read through the book. Although many of his experiences were similar, his reasons for flying were different. You can fill in some of these reasons on the bottom line, like the example shown.

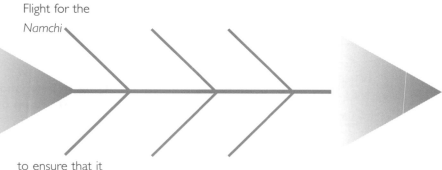

Flight for the *Namchi*

to ensure that it set sail with Di Chou before the wedding

Hang in there, Judy!

Flying the wind may be exhilarating, but even if it's your chosen sport it is not without its dangers. Judy Leden, many times world champion of hang-gliding and paragliding, describes her experience of hang-gliding at 40,000 feet above Jordan, after being released from a hot air balloon:

'Fly, please fly!'

The air didn't catch me, but eventually it stopped rotating... At last it responded and with a smooth surge, it pitched upwards. My oxygen cylinder 'pinged' clear of the wires and I was flying.

The rush of relief was immediately replaced by pain. The wind whipped up under my visor making my eyes water. I blinked and immediately my eyelashes froze together and I couldn't see anything. I was flying at the same height as commercial airliners and was completely blind! I felt the skin on my face burn with cold as my flesh froze...

Judy is writing in her autobiography, *Flying with Condors*. Talking directly to us as she experiences some hair-raising flights, we feel as if we are on a rollercoaster, joining her as she battles against danger. However, as a writer she does not use the sort of sentence structure or vocabulary that a fiction writer needs to involve his or her readers.

Spot the difference

Here is a similar extract from *The Kite Rider*. Compare the different way in which we feel for Haoyou as he flies.

◉   How does Geraldine McCaughrean involve us in his flight?
◉   Discuss the following when you have read the passage:
  • sentence variety
  • use of verbs
  • figurative language.

Wind rushed past his ears in a deafening bluster. Then stillness. His stomach rose into his throat. The kite began to fall. Below him, the sailors stopped paying out rope and gave a tug. It flexed Haoyou's spine like the cracking of a whip. A pain like a bolt of lightning went through his head and shot down the tendons of his legs.

(pages 48–49)

> **Taking to the air?** One of the latest crazes is kite-surfing (proving particularly popular in Wales). Why not try some of the kite-surfing websites to learn more about this exhilarating sport?

Agony Aunt Special

Sun Swallow and his voice, 'Tongue of Fire', will put you in touch with the spirits of your ancestors!

Here are some letters from the residents of Yangcun – they want some answers from Sun Swallow 'translated' by his Tongue of Fire, Mipeng.

Did Hop Li Yung poison my chickens?

Dear Mipeng

My family keep chickens, not just for ourselves but also for our neighbours. In return we get silk, vegetables, rice. Our neighbour, Hop Li Yung, also keeps chickens... miserable, scraggy birds not worth a cash. I have seen him shouting at ours, trying to run them mad. Now some of them are sick and I think he has been feeding them poisoned scraps. What do the spirits want me to do? I have a wife and two worthless daughters to keep.

Yours in hope

JH

Dear JH

The spirits of your ancestors tell me that you should offer them chicken meat and give some also to Hop Li Yung.

If he has poisoned your chickens, he will not want to eat their meat! Then you must accuse him of having shamed your ancestors who have already eaten the poisoned meat. In this way he will be shunned all his neighbours and bring shame on himself.

If he accepts the meat you will have made a friend; but you must stop him from eating it, saying that it is unworthy of his friendship.

Offer him instead many portions of rice. It is obvious with such scrawny birds that he does not have enough food to feed his family.

Yours

Mipeng

Breathe some fire...

Sound out Mipeng's 'tongue of fire' for yourself by using this glossary.

cash – ancient Chinese coins of less value than *tael* (see below)

worthless daughters – girls were not valued in the past, since they did not financially support the family

spirits of your ancestors – the Chinese believe that family members who die watch over them and guide them

partake – to join in something or eat something (take part)

denounce – to tell everyone that a person has done something wrong, to accuse or inform

shun – to avoid or ignore someone deliberately

unworthy – not deserving something

tael – ancient Chinese money

Who did Chang want to inherit the business?

Dear Mipeng,

I work on the river barges with two companions. We were paid by the merchant, Chang, a wealthy man. He died last month and his widow says that he left a chest full of tael to support all the equipment we have to buy for repairs and maintenance. His widow used to keep the books for him.

My companion Lin Po wants to marry his widow and says that Chang intended the business to go to him because he knew that his wife would be looked after. But our other companion Ming Ti Chep says he'll see Lin dead first.

Now Ming Ti Chep has disappeared...what should I do?

Yours in desperation

SY

Dear SY

You must be careful.

The spirits of your ancestors tell you to beware of Lin Po. You must speak to the head of your family and ask him to go with you to the magistrate and tell what you know.

Your ancestors say that the spirit of Ming Ti Chep is with them and you should not delay.

Do not speak to Chang's widow or Lin Po but go with all haste.

Yours

Mipeng

Mimicking Mipeng

The Yangcun peasants have plenty of other questions for Haoyou and Mipeng in the novel. Some examples would be:

- Did Great-Grandfather Xian leave a buried chest of *tael* that no one has managed to find?
- Is my husband still angry with me for arguing with him just before he died?
- Did someone kidnap my twin baby boys because they only had girls?

- With one of you in role as Mipeng, use the style of the letters to discuss the stories behind the questions on page 80 of the novel.
- Work out an answer for Mipeng. Remember to speak as Mipeng would. Use the glossary on page 10 to help you.
- Share some of the answers with other pairs and discuss whether Mipeng's advice would work.

Did you know?

Many Chinese still believe that the spirits of their ancestors will look after them if they are properly respected by daily prayers and offerings to an altar or shrine.

Quick Quiz

Haoyou sees his father's spirit when he is flying a kite. True or false? (This question might test your powers of prediction!)

THE KITE RIDER

Quest for Romance

The handsome prince...

The figure of the Great Miao is set against the colourful background of the Jade Circus and a noble tradition of Emperor Dynasties.

- ◉ If you had to draw a picture of Miao, what would he be like?
- ◉ Draw his portrait outline and pin it up on a wall.
- ◉ Search for more information about him in *The Kite Rider* and finish your portrait.

Here are some clues to set you on your trail:

dressed entirely in white, except for a green silk scarf around his throat (page 58)

his scrupulous cleanliness (page 71)

equipped to put back Haoyou's dislocated shoulder into its socket (page 99)

the Miao was oddly agitated (page 104)

such cat-like softness (page 111)

a stalactite, an icicle (page 170)

Haoyou felt awkward. He felt oddly in the way, like an interpreter between two foreigners. (page 77)

'It is unforgivable to insult a man's kin.' (page 124)

'For the last year... I have been on a journey of discovery.' (page 126)

The Miao glanced down at the unaccustomed feel of a hand clasping his. (page 84)

so pale, so listless, mesmerized (page 133)

his face contorted once again with inner agony (page 137)

'You see what you've done?' she berated him (page 126)

she said abstractedly that she wanted to keep the circus master in sight (page 131)

'What have I done?' he groaned. (page 161)

She had actually leaned over and *put her hand over the royal mouth*! And yet the circus master did not appear to mind. (page 144)

He saw indistinctly two shapes merge, as Miao Jié put an arm around Mipeng. (page 165

His Cinderella?

Mipeng is an unlikely candidate, surely? She's 'Tall and leaning, like a weary heron'. What do you think is the attraction? What draws Miao to confide in her?

Look for more clues by reading around the excerpts above.

Simply Inspirational!

Romance is not just in the growing love between two characters, but in the language of the novel, its structure and settings.

When the 13th-century traveller, Marco Polo returned to his native Venice, he brought back tales of Kublai Khan and his summer palace in Xanadu. This inspired artists and writers to search for and recreate the wonders seen there, such as the poem *Kubla Khan* by Samuel Taylor Coleridge.

In Xanadu did Kubla Khan
A stately pleasure-dome decree:
Where Alph, the sacred river, ran
Through caverns measureless to man
Down to a sunless sea.

Seeing is believing...

For Haoyou, the name Xanadu 'was rich with mystery and promise... the lair of Kublai Khan himself'. When he finally sees the Khan, although not at Xanadu, he is in a similarly exotic setting.

The Khan's yurt was made from otter and marmot and ermine furs, hung with cloth of beaten gold and panels of painted silk, and the floor was strewn with tiger skins. Porcelain vases of cobalt blue and dazzling white stood on tables of lacquered black-and-gold... [Amid this sat the Khan on] a couch of plush magnificence.   (page 132)

- ◉ Pick out words or phrases that appeal most to your senses.
- ◉ What is especially exotic or unusual in this paragraph? (Look at the nouns, noun phrases and adjectives.)
- ◉ Much of the description is written in the passive voice. What effect does this have?

A lost city?

At the end of the 1980s, when still a student, the travel writer, William Dalrymple set off with his girlfriend on a quest to find Xanadu. In communist China, this proved something of an adventure.

We drove into the ruined city and headed for the inner enclosure, the Jeep slipping in the mud. ... There was no sign of the marble palace, the gilt rooms or the lovely murals... Instead, through the pelting rain we saw the shattered foundations of pavilions and temples, with column bases, capitals, roof tiles and pottery fragments littering the ground.

Look again at the points you noted about Haoyou's sighting of the Khan.
- ◉ What are the main differences with this extract?
- ◉ What is the effect of Dalrymple using the active voice?

Search for Xanadu

Struggles for Freedom

What do You Know about China?

Think of China and what comes to mind? Fried rice and spring rolls? Cheap clothes or exotic silk? A language of symbols?

Cut off for centuries from the West and now with a sixth of the world's population, China (or Cathay as it *was* referred to) is still a mysterious and undiscovered country. Check out our file on China to find out more…

Watch this space…
Today China is opening up and set to dominate the world stage as Western business rushes to its cities. Conscious of their image, its youth embrace Western fashion and technology while retaining the enigmatic Chinese spirit.

Inscrutable…
One of the world's most ancient civilisations, China's history goes back to 6,000 BC under the rule of dynasties governed by kings and later emperors.

Divide and rule…
As we have learned from the Mighty Khan's invasion, the Chinese constantly struggled to repel enemies and the Great Wall was built to keep out invaders. The states *within* China also fought each other and dynasties only survived through the strong, and often terrorizing, hand of government.

Inspirational…
Yet Chinese culture is based on a discipline of respect, obedience, patience and an appreciation of others. Chinese religions and philosophies have been adopted by Westerners to emulate this spirit of peace and serenity.

A question of character?

The characters in *The Kite Rider* display many typical Chinese characteristics.

- Match the quotes and names below.
- Decide whether they show any of the qualities listed in the information on China above.

dressed in Chinese robes… speaking in excellent Mandarin Chinese
(page 132)

quiet-spoken at the best of times
(page 24)

'To submit to Fate. That's a kind of obedience too'
(page 142)

'She kept her eyes determinedly on her sewing.'
(page 163)

Mipeng   Miao Jié   The Mighty Khan   Auntie Mo   Qing'an

'I weep for your sorrows'
(page 13)

 Do *you* have any of these 'Chinese' characteristics? Working with a partner, give each other a score of 1 to 10.

From Turbulent Past to Challenging Future

After years of cruel oppression by the emperors, Mao Zedong led the Chinese communists into revolution and seized power in 1947. This created another oppressive regime, and even now China is struggling to combine a more democratic society with communist ideals.

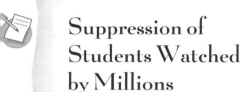

Suppression of Students Watched by Millions

In 1989 a student protest in Tiananmen Square, Beijing, resulted in the army opening fire and massacring demonstrators.

This poem by James Fenton was amongst many responses to events in Tiananmen Square.

Tiananmen
Is broad and clean
And you can't tell
Where the dead have been
And you can't tell
What happened then
And you can't speak
Of Tiananmen

by James Fenton (Hong Kong, 15 June 1989)

Focus on Jung Chang

Raised in the privileged circles of China's communist society, Jung Chang saw Chairman Mao as a liberator, and initially became a member of the Red Army. Eventually disillusioned by a regime of terror, she escaped to Britain where she wrote the highly successful *Wild Swans* which tells the story of three generations of her family.

Women, men and families

The struggles of Jung Chang's mother and grandmother (as well as her own) are similar to those depicted in *The Kite Rider*. Like Haoyou, Jung Chang's love, respect and admiration for her family are the main strengths of her survival.

One day I heard my father telling my mother about a compliment paid to her by one of his colleagues, whose wife had the reputation of being a beauty. 'The two of us are lucky to have such outstanding wives,' he had said to my father. … My father was beaming... 'I smiled politely, of course,' he said. 'But I was really thinking, How can you compare your wife with mine? My wife is in a class of her own!'

⊙ Find a passage in *The Kite Rider* that describes the relationship between Gou Pei and Qing'an.

⊙ Discuss with a partner what effect this had on Haoyou's struggle for his family.

Pathw.ays. . . to Another Good Read

Works by the same author

Plundering Paradise
by Geraldine McCaughrean

(ISBN 0-19-271876-2)

This novel centres around pirates in Madagascar and is another rollercoaster of fun, colour and adventure.

Gold Dust **by Geraldine McCaughrean**

(ISBN 0-19-275359-2)

Caught up in a gold rush, this is a story about two children trying to defend their home – a pacy and funny adventure.

The Stones are Hatching
by Geraldine McCaughrean

(ISBN 0-19-275091-7)

A lyrical fantasy adventure and the story of a quest to save the world!

Fiction by other authors

Tightrope **by Gillian Cross**

(ISBN 0-19-271750-2)

This novel has you on the edge of your seat as a teenager is poised on the knife-edge of crime.

Xtreme: Edge v. 1 (Xtreme) **by Ben Bo**

(ISBN 0-74-754581-2)

An exciting snow boarding thriller.

Feather Boy **by Nicky Singer Collins**

(ISBN 0-00-712026-5)

A moving novel about loyalty, survival and finding yourself.

Journey to the River Sea **by Eva Ibbotson**

(ISBN 0-58-279592-3)

The tale of the journey of an orphaned London schoolgirl and her formidable governess to South America – a colourful adventure in which the Amazon rainforest meets *The Little Princess!*

Books about China

China **by Noelle Morris**

(ISBN 1-84-421317-X)

Your Travel Guide to Ancient China
by Josepha Sherman

(ISBN 0-82-253073-2)

Red Scarf Girl **by Ji-Li Jiang**

(ISBN 0-06-446208-0)

This is an autobiography looking at the persecution of Ji-Li Jiang's family during the Cultural Revolution, and the difficult decisions she had to make.

If you'd like to know more about kites and how to make them, try:

Kites and Kite Flying
by Ambrose Lloyd and Nicolette Thomas

(ISBN 0-60-035337-0)

The book contains a full history of kite making and flying, and instructions on how to make six of the most popular.